YOUNG OBSERVER

BLACK HOLES
and other space phenomena

Philip Steele

SCHOLASTIC INC.
New York Toronto London Auckland Sydney
Mexico City New Delhi Hong Kong

ISBN 0-439-13368-8

Text copyright © 1995 by Larousse plc.
Illustrations copyright © 1995 by Larousse plc.
Design copyright © 1995 by David West Children's Books.
All rights reserved. Published by Scholastic Inc., 555 Broadway, New York, NY 10012, by arrangement with Larousse Kingfisher Chambers Inc.

SCHOLASTIC and associated logos are trademarks and/or registered trademarks of Scholastic Inc.

12 11 10 9 8 7 6 5 4 3 2 1   9/9 0 1 2 3 4/0

Printed in the U.S.A.   14

First Scholastic printing, October 1998

Conceived and created by

David West • CHILDREN'S BOOKS

Author: Philip Steele
Consultants: Carole Stott, Ian Graham
Cover illustrations: Ian Thompson and Rob Shone
Illustrations: Ian Thompson
Line illustrations: Rob Shone

CONTENTS

INTRODUCTION

Why are there gigantic black holes in the depths of space? What would happen if a great chunk of space rock smashed into the Earth? When will the Sun stop shining? Why do some stars explode and others fade away? How do astronauts prepare their breakfast on the space shuttle?

The more we find out about space, the more questions there are to ask. This is the book to answer them....

It visits our neighbors, the planets and their moons. It embarks on journeys into deep space, seeking out supernovas and pulsars, giving the latest information on rockets, satellites, and space probes.

There are dozens of fascinating facts in this book. You can test what you've read—and some of what you may already know—with the Young Observer trivia quiz at the end of each chapter. If you get stuck, the answers are in the back.

CHAPTER ONE

HEAVENLY BODIES

Red giants, white dwarfs, black holes, and galaxies... They are all out there, deep in the starry night sky.

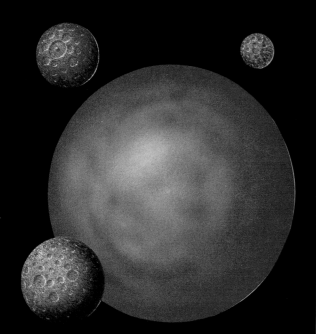

But what are they? And what do they look like? Read on, to explore some of the mysteries that are lurking in the dark depths of outer space.

ANCIENT EGYPTIAN and Chinese *astronomers* looked up at the night sky and studied the stars with as much wonder and awe as we do today. But their understanding of space was very different from ours. In fact, it wasn't until 400 years ago that people began to accept that our planet Earth is round. Before this time, most people thought that the world was flat...

The ancient Egyptians believed the night sky was the body of a goddess called Nut. Her star-spangled body arched over the Earth.

...and that if sailors went on long journeys they were in danger of falling off the edge!

ARISTOTLE, the ancient Greek thinker, realized that the Earth must be round as early as the 330s B.C. He was watching an *eclipse* when he noticed that the Earth was casting a round shadow on the face of the Moon. Aristotle believed that the other planets and the Sun all travel around the Earth.

GALILEO (1564–1642), the great Italian *astronomer*, studied the sky through the newly-invented *telescope* and became convinced that the Earth travels around the Sun, not the Sun around the Earth. This went against the teachings of the Church, and so Galileo was put on trial.

TODAY, people are still arguing about outer space. The most popular theory about the creation of the *universe* is that it began with a vast explosion about 15 billion years ago. *Cosmologists* have named this the BIG BANG theory.

After the BIG BANG, the universe kept expanding and is still getting bigger today. Some cosmologists think that the universe will stop expanding and shrink back to nothing in the BIG CRUNCH!

NEW MATTER FORMING

NEW GALAXIES FORMING

OLD GALAXIES

UNIVERSE EXPANDING

THE UNIVERSE contains as many as 100 billion billion stars, grouped together in gigantic "star-cities" called *galaxies*. The Big Bang sent the young universe flying out in all directions, and even today the galaxies—and everything in them—are still rushing away from each other at high speed. As the universe grows, galaxies are still forming on its far edges.

THE MILKY WAY

is the name we have given to our own galaxy. It contains about 1,000 billion stars, of which the Sun is just one. We can see it from Earth, as a band of milky-white light across the sky. Out in space, viewed from above, it looks like a gigantic whirlpool with spiraling arms. Sideways on, it's a bit like two fried eggs stuck together!

The Milky Way (a spiral galaxy) viewed from the side.

Irregular galaxy

Elliptical galaxy

Barred-spiral galaxy

COUNTLESS OTHER GALAXIES lie beyond ours, stretching out into deepest space. Nobody knows exactly how many there are—perhaps as many as 100 billion. Not all of these galaxies are spiral-shaped. Elliptical galaxies are rounded or oval, while irregular galaxies have no special shape at all. Each new galaxy that is discovered is given a number—and sometimes its own name as well. M104 has been nicknamed the Sombrero, because it looks a little like a big Mexican hat, and the bright, swirling M51 galaxy is known as the Whirlpool!

Most galaxies are so far away from Earth that they can only be seen through extremely powerful telescopes. These telescopes are like giant cameras that take photographs of the sky— astronomers do not look through them directly!

STARS ARE BORN in a great cloud of hydrogen gas and dust called a *nebula*. This begins to break up and shrink into spinning balls. Then each ball becomes so incredibly hot in its center that *nuclear reactions* are triggered, and the hydrogen starts to turn into another gas called helium. The young star now glows brightly and gives off vast amounts of heat.

1. Our Sun was born in a cold, dark nebula cloud.

2. Stars formed from the nebula.

3. At first the Sun was a cool star.

4. The Sun is now at this stage of its life.

The Sun might seem huge to us, but it is only a medium-sized star. It has been shining for about 4.6 billion years and is about halfway through its life. Its surface is a super-hot cauldron of bubbling gases and great tongues of flame!

THE BIGGEST stars are called *giants*, and they can have 20 or 30 times as much gas in them as our Sun. They blaze brightly, but soon burn up their gas fuel. Small, dim stars are called *dwarfs*. The brightness of the stars we see from Earth depends on their size and how far away they are from us.

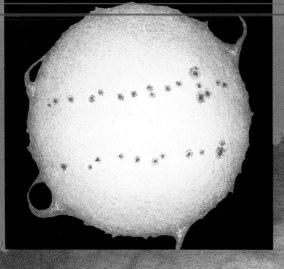

Supergiant

A RED GIANT is an old star that has swollen to many times its normal size. This final blaze of glory happens when the star's helium *core* collapses and gets hot enough to blow its hydrogen up into a vast orange-red ball. The biggest stars may swell into **supergiants**, 2,000 times the size of our Sun.

5. Toward the end of its life, the Sun will swell into a red giant.

Really massive stars—at least eight times the size of the Sun—don't fade slowly. They go out with an almighty bang and look like a bright, new star. Exploding stars are called **supernovas**.

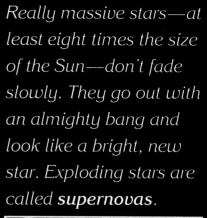

A WHITE DWARF is almost the final stage in a star's life. The gas surface of the red giant is blown off, and the star is now a planetary nebula. In the center of the gas shell is the red giant's hot, shrunken core—a white dwarf star. Over billions of years, this fades into a cinder and dies.

— *7. A white dwarf*

6. A planetary nebula

A black hole would suck in any passing spacecraft within a millionth of a second! Even nearby stars would be gulped up. A giant black hole may lurk at the center of our own galaxy, the Milky Way.

BLACK HOLES are one of the greatest mysteries of space. We cannot see them, and astronomers only know they exist because of their effect on nearby stars. They happen sometimes after a star blows up in a supernova. The star's *gravity* pulls all the material that remains after the explosion inward, squeezing it smaller and smaller. Either a tiny *neutron star* forms or a black hole—an object with such strong gravity that nothing can escape from it, not even light.

PULSARS are neutron stars that spin round and round, giving off a narrow beam of light and radio waves which sweeps through space like a lighthouse beacon. When these rapid pulses of energy were first detected in 1967, astronomers were baffled. Some thought they were hearing messages from aliens!

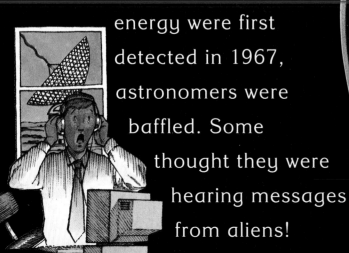

TWIN STARS are called binaries. These stars spend their lives *orbiting* each other, held together by the pull of each other's gravity. Although the two stars were probably born at the same time, they are often completely different in color and brightness. Around a quarter of the stars in our galaxy are binaries.

COMETS are giant snowballs made of snow and dust. They *orbit* the Sun, but only a few ever come close to it. If they do, the heat starts to melt them and they grow long tails of gas and dust.

MILLIONS OF ASTEROIDS

orbit the Sun in a belt between the planets Mars and Jupiter. Asteroids are minor planets that come in many different sizes. Many are no larger than a house, but there is a huge asteroid called Ceres which measures around 580 miles across.

Some people think that the dinosaurs died out after a huge meteorite hit the Earth, sending up a cloud of dust that blocked out the Sun and fatally changed the climate.

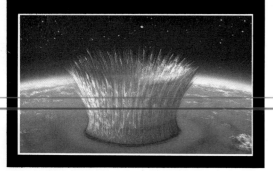

SHOOTING STARS

or *meteors* are light trails created by tiny space rocks burning up as they speed toward the Earth. Larger pieces that survive to crash into the ground are called *meteorites*. No one is known to have been seriously hurt by a meteorite, but somebody in New York State had a close shave in 1993—he found that a meteorite had smashed a hole right through his car!

The **Young Observer** *Quiz*

1. How many Earths will fit into the Sun?

a) 50?

b) 250,000?

c) 1,300,000?

2. How hot is the Sun?

a) 10,000 °F?

b) 27 million °F?

c) 250 million °F?

3. How fast can a comet travel?

a) 15,000 miles per hour?

b) 150,000 miles per hour?

c) 1,500,000 miles per hour?

4. What's the heaviest surviving meteorite to have hit the Earth?

a) 6 tons?

b) 60 tons?

c) 600 tons?

5. Where are we in this picture of our galaxy?

a) ?

b) ?

c) ?

6. How many asteroids are there?

a) 5,000?

b) 500,000?

c) Millions?

7. What is a light-year?

a) A year with lots of sunshine?

b) The distance light travels in one year?

c) Earth's distance from the Sun?

8. Where can you find a horse's head in space?

a) In a spaceship?

b) On the Moon?

c) In a nebula?

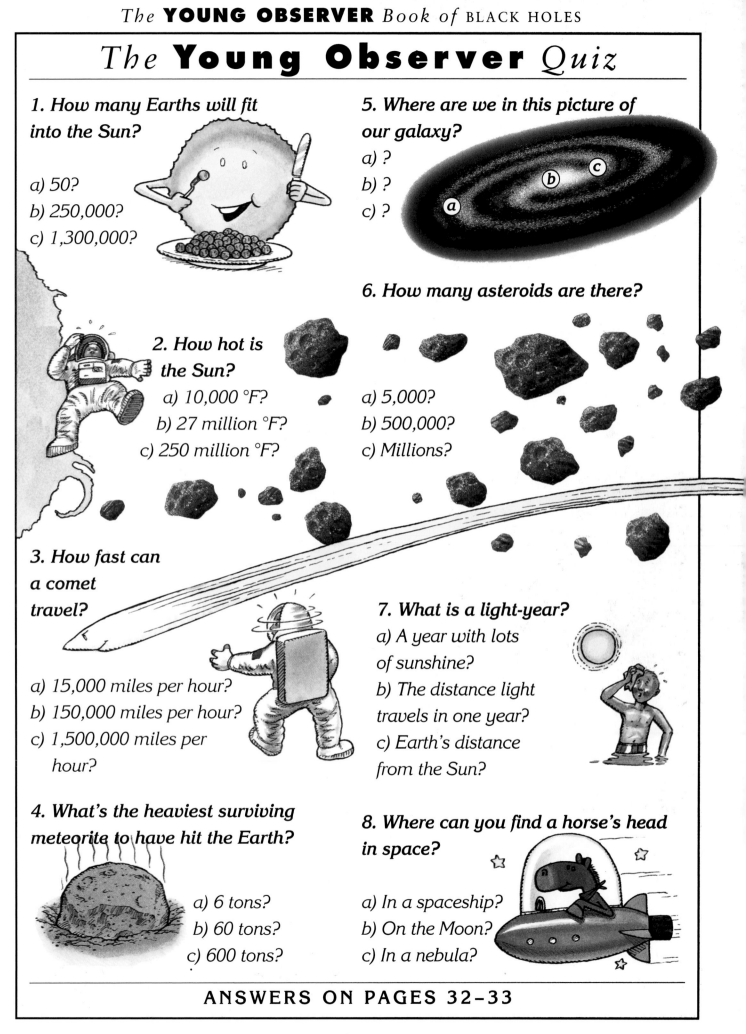

ANSWERS ON PAGES 32–33

CHAPTER TWO

OUR FAMILY OF PLANETS

Gigantic volcanoes, red deserts, yellow skies, lonely moons....
Our neighbors, the eight planets, are strange and mysterious worlds— observed by space probes, but not yet explored.

Why do the planets travel around our star, the Sun? When were they born? Could people live on any planet other than Earth?

THE SOLAR SYSTEM is the name given to the Sun and all the space bodies that move around it —from the nine planets and their moons, to *asteroids* and *comets*. These space bodies are all held in their orbits by the enormous pull of the Sun's gravity. Without this, everything would spin away into outer space.

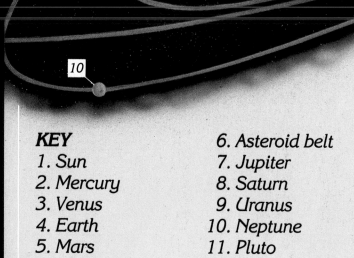

11

8

10

KEY
1. Sun
2. Mercury
3. Venus
4. Earth
5. Mars
6. Asteroid belt
7. Jupiter
8. Saturn
9. Uranus
10. Neptune
11. Pluto

THE PLANETS were formed from the leftovers of the nebula that gave birth to the Sun. They aren't as big or as hot as stars, and they cannot make light of their own. They reflect the Sun's light.

6

9

4

1

3

7

2

5

PLANETS SPIN LIKE TOPS as they orbit the Sun. The time a planet takes to spin around once on its **axis** is called its period of rotation. The time it takes to travel around the Sun is its orbital period. As the planets move through space,

Axis

most are orbited in turn—by spinning moons.

Some time after the Sun was born, a huge, spinning doughnut-shaped cloud of gas and dust took shape around it. The dust clumped together, forming the rocky planets. From the gas came the four giant gas planets.

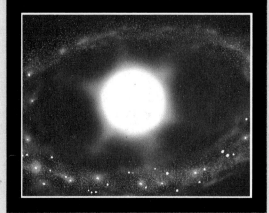

MERCURY has been battered and bashed by so many asteroids, comets, and meteorites that its surface is scarred with craters. This small planet is the closest to the Sun, and every day there is a heat wave, with temperatures soaring as high as 800 °F. Mercury hasn't enough *atmosphere* to hold in heat, so nights drop to –290 °F, about three times as cold as the lowest temperature recorded on Earth. Mercury rotates slowly— once every 58 Earth-days 16 hours.

VENUS was the goddess of love in ancient Rome, but the planet named after her is far from lovely. Poisonous yellow clouds blanket its rocky surface, trapping the Sun's heat and making Venus the hottest planet —its temperature reaches 900 °F. Acid rain falls from the clouds and lightning flickers between them. There may also be active volcanoes in its high mountain ranges.

Lightning flickers across Venus's murky, yellow sky.

OUR HOME PLANET,

Earth has sparkling blue oceans and is wreathed in white clouds. It is the only planet to have oxygen (the gas that all animals need to breathe to stay alive) in its atmosphere. And it is just the right distance from the Sun for it to be neither too hot nor too cold to support an amazing variety of plant and animal life.

New moon

Crescent

OUR MOON is an airless ball of rock. The Sun

only lights one half at a time—the other half is in darkness. And because the Moon only spins once on its axis in the 27 Earth-days 7 hours it takes to travel around the Earth, we always see the same face. The Moon appears to change its shape during its orbit because we see different parts of its sunlit half at different times.

First quarter

Gibbous moon

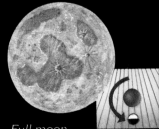

Full moon

Wide plains, craters, and high mountain ranges make shadowy patterns on the face of the Moon. People often think the patterns look like a face —thus the stories about the Man in the Moon!

Mars

Jupiter has a spotty face! Telescopes show a strange marking called the Great Red Spot, so big that two Earths could fit inside. It is a gigantic hurricane that has been raging for at least 300 years.

Jupiter

Europa (one of Jupiter's moons)

MARS is only half the size of the Earth. Imagine a desert world covered in red rocks and dunes, under a pink, dusty sky. One of Mars's volcanoes, Olympus Mons,

Ganymede (Jupiter's largest moon)

is the tallest in the **solar system** (three times as high as Mount Everest), while the planet is seamed by huge gorges— also far bigger than any on Earth. These make patterns on the surface of Mars which can be seen from Earth. Some astronomers used to think that the gorges were canal-like structures, built by Martians. But **space probes** have yet to find any sign of life there!

JUPITER is the biggest planet in the solar system. It is 11 times the size of Earth and contains over 300 times as much material. At its center is a small, rocky *core*, but the bulk of the planet is made up of hydrogen. Violent storm clouds swirl through its atmosphere, which is streaked by flashes of lightning. Jupiter may be a giant, but it is still the fastest spinner of all the planets, rotating once every 9 Earth-hours 55 minutes.

Saturn

The other three gas giants also have rings, but Saturn's are the brightest and most spectacular. They are made up of pieces of rock, ice, and dust.

SATURN has the most moons—18 at the last count—and many people think that its broad, glistening rings make it the most beautiful planet. Like its neighbor, Jupiter, Saturn is a gas giant, with a small, rocky core surrounded by hydrogen. It, too, has terrible storms and high winds. Although Saturn is the second largest planet, it is so light that it would actually float in water!

URANUS was the first planet to be discovered with a telescope—in 1781. Space probes have shown us that it has 11 narrow rings and 15 moons. Its atmosphere is a blue-green blanket of methane gas, with an ocean of hydrogen and a rocky core beneath it.

Uranus has flipped! Most planets have a slightly tilted axis, but Uranus is on its side. At some point it must have been tipped over—perhaps by a large asteroid.

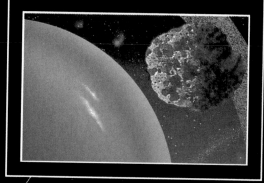

NEPTUNE is too far away for astronomers to see it clearly from Earth, even through powerful telescopes. It was known to have two moons before 1989, when Voyager 2 revealed another six!

Neptune

Uranus

PLUTO is a tiny frozen planet, with a moon called Charon which is half its size. Both are thought to be icy balls of rock and frozen methane. Pluto wasn't discovered until 1930, after years of scientific detective work.

Pluto

The **Young Observer** *Quiz*

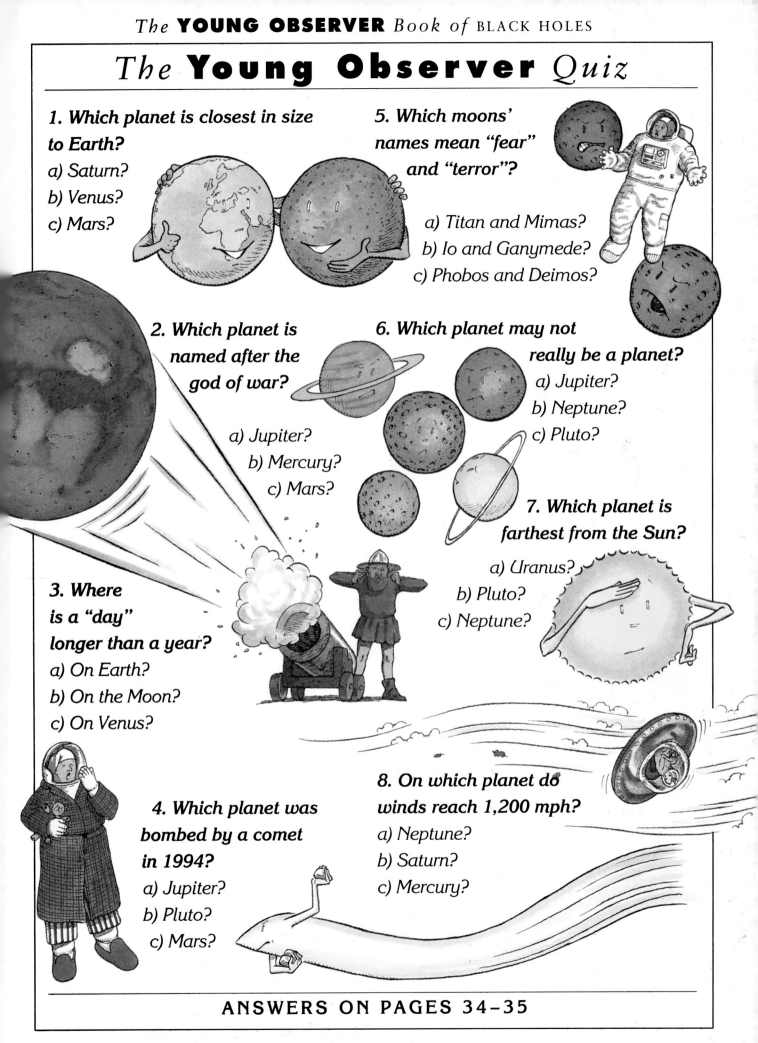

1. Which planet is closest in size to Earth?
a) Saturn?
b) Venus?
c) Mars?

5. Which moons' names mean "fear" and "terror"?
a) Titan and Mimas?
b) Io and Ganymede?
c) Phobos and Deimos?

2. Which planet is named after the god of war?
a) Jupiter?
b) Mercury?
c) Mars?

6. Which planet may not really be a planet?
a) Jupiter?
b) Neptune?
c) Pluto?

3. Where is a "day" longer than a year?
a) On Earth?
b) On the Moon?
c) On Venus?

7. Which planet is farthest from the Sun?
a) Uranus?
b) Pluto?
c) Neptune?

4. Which planet was bombed by a comet in 1994?
a) Jupiter?
b) Pluto?
c) Mars?

8. On which planet do winds reach 1,200 mph?
a) Neptune?
b) Saturn?
c) Mercury?

ANSWERS ON PAGES 34–35

CHAPTER THREE

VIKINGS AND OTHER VOYAGERS

This century we have embarked on the greatest adventure in our history— the exploration of the solar system!

Rockets, satellites, space probes, and stations.... How do they work, what missions have they accomplished, and what are their destinations?

THE CHINESE were making firework *rockets* 900 years ago. They were powered by black powder, an early kind of gunpowder. In 1903 a Russian scientist called Konstantin Tsiolkovsky worked out how to use liquid fuels to power rockets.

AN AMERICAN scientist named Robert Goddard launched the first liquid-fuel rocket in 1926. It was nearly 12 feet long and it burned gasoline and liquid oxygen. This created a jet of gas that lifted the rocket 40 feet.

Goddard and his rocket

SPUTNIK 1 was launched by the U.S.S.R. on October 4, 1957. It was the first artificial satellite ever to be sent into space. It stayed in orbit for 3 months before burning up.

SPACE ROCKETS were developed in the U.S.A. and U.S.S.R. (now Russia), during the 1950s. At first they were used to launch artificial **satellites** into orbit around the Earth. A rocket has to reach a speed of at least 7 miles per second before it can escape the pull of Earth's gravity. That's 80 times the speed of the world's fastest train!

Sputnik 1

Yuri Gagarin

Valentina Tereshkova

The first person to walk in space was the cosmonaut (Russian astronaut) Aleksei Leonov, on March 18, 1965. He was outside his spacecraft for 20 minutes.

THE FIRST MAN IN SPACE was Yuri Gagarin, a Russian who orbited the Earth in Vostok 1, on April 12, 1961. The first woman, Valentina Tereshkova, took off in Vostok 6 in 1963.

Command module

Service module

Lunar module

3rd stage rocket

2nd stage rocket

1st stage rocket

USA

THE FIRST SUCCESSFUL MOON LANDING took place on July 20, 1969, when U.S. astronauts Neil Armstrong and Buzz Aldrin became the first people to set foot on the Moon. A huge three-stage Saturn 5 rocket had blasted off from Earth four days earlier, carrying a spacecraft that had three sections called modules. While the Command and Service modules orbited the Moon, the Lunar Module traveled down to its surface. There were five more Moon landings, during which astronauts carried out experiments and collected rock and soil samples for analysis back on Earth.

A third crew member, Michael Collins, stayed in orbit while the other two traveled down to the Moon's surface.

A U.S. flag flies on the Moon. Or does it? The Moon has no air and therefore no wind. In fact, the flag in the famous pictures was held up by wire!

UNITED STATES

SPACE STATIONS are designed to stay in orbit around the Earth for long periods of time, so that astronauts and cosmonauts can live and work in space. Smaller spacecraft can dock with the station, bringing up fresh crews. Skylab was a U.S. station in orbit from 1973 to 1979. Mir is a Russian station, launched in 1986.

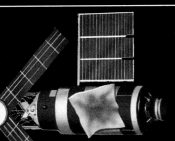

Skylab

Mir space station

Docking port

Solar panels turn sunlight into electricity

Working and living quarters

RETURNING TO EARTH is dangerous.

The atmosphere around our planet burns up most objects that travel through it. Capsules containing astronauts are protected by heat shields. Parachutes slow the capsule as it nears the Earth's surface.

One Russian cosmonaut has lived in space for over a year. Things are virtually weightless in space, so they float about unless held down. Long periods of weightlessness can weaken muscles and bones.

THE SPACE SHUTTLE is a U.S. spacecraft that can be reused. It is launched by rockets, and then goes into orbit around the Earth. When it returns to the ground, it glides down and lands on a runway. The shuttle orbiter may be used to release satellites into space, or to capture and repair them. Or it may carry a small laboratory called Spacelab in its cargo bay, where crews conduct experiments. Astronauts can use jet-powered backpacks called MMUs to move around outside the craft.

A crew member uses an MMU (manned maneuvering unit) to space walk and guide a damaged satellite onto the shuttle orbiter's long manipulator arm. The satellite will be pulled into the cargo bay for repair.

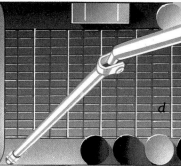

3. The main fuel tank drops away and breaks up on reentry.

2a. The booster rockets fall away.

1. The shuttle takes off, using liquid fuel from a main tank and two solid-fuel booster rockets.

2b. The boosters parachute back to Earth, for reuse.

KEY

a) Flight deck
b) Air lock
c) Manipulator arm
d) Cargo bay
e) Cargo bay doors
f) Crew member with MMU
g) Rescued satellite

h) Landing gear
i) Fuel tanks
j) Main engines
k) Orbiter engines
l) Thrusters for maneuvering

BURAN is a Russian shuttle which was launched by powerful Energia rockets on November 15, 1988. It was controlled by computers and did not have a crew. Unmanned missions may save lives, but some problems are best solved by people on the spot.

4. The shuttle orbiter goes into Earth orbit, cruising at 17,300 mph.

5. The orbiter turns around and fires rockets to slow down.

6. The orbiter maneuvers into reentry position.

7. The orbiter reenters Earth's atmosphere. Heatproof tiles prevent it from burning up.

8. The orbiter glides back toward the landing site.

9. The orbiter lands on the runway at about 200 mph.

g

c

f

l

i

k

h

j

k

l

Communications satellite

Weather satellite

Landsat

Seasat

ARTIFICIAL SATELLITES have come a long way since the Sputnik days. Communications satellites now bounce radio, television, and telephone signals around our planet. Military satellites can spy and guide missiles. Weather satellites track hurricanes and help with forecasting. Other satellites map the land and the oceans, and collect information on the environment. Yet others gaze beyond the solar system, to discover the secrets of deep space.

Space is littered with junk! There are bits and pieces of broken satellites, old tools, and other debris. And that's dangerous. At the speeds reached by the shuttle, even a speck of paint is a serious hazard.

Hubble Space Telescope

THE HUBBLE SPACE TELESCOPE orbits the Earth at a height of 360 miles and gives us unique views of distant parts of the universe. When it was first launched in

1990, its "eyesight" was a bit faulty—the pictures it sent back to Earth were fuzzy. It was repaired in 1993, by astronauts space-walking from the space shuttle *Endeavour*. As well as mending or replacing various instruments and controls, the astronauts managed to fit a set of mirrors which work a bit like glasses to correct Hubble's eyesight.

Ulysses

SPACE PROBES can be speeded on their way by using the pull of another planet's gravity. The Ulysses probe was launched in 1990 and passed Jupiter in 1992, using its gravity to swing onto a path that took it over the Sun's *poles* in 1994 and 1995.

GIOTTO was launched in 1985 to study Halley's Comet, and in 1986 passed within 370 miles of its core. The space probe was battered by comet dust, but it still sent back images that allowed scientists to work out that the core measured 10 miles by 5 miles.

In 1992 Giotto investigated the comet Grigg-Skjellerup.

FANTASTIC VOYAGES of discovery have been carried out by unmanned space probes. Russian Venera probes parachuted down to the surface of Venus in the 1960s to 1980s, and managed to send back pictures before being destroyed by the planet's atmosphere. Back in 1976, the U.S.A.'s two Viking probes dropped landers on Mars. The U.S.A.'s Cassini probe is to be launched toward Saturn in the late 1990s. It will drop a mini-probe by parachute to study the atmosphere of Saturn's largest moon, Titan.

Viking space probe

FLY-BY PROBES zip around the planets, taking pictures as they pass. The U.S.A.'s Mariners spied on Venus, Mars, and Mercury in the 1960s and 1970s. But the superstars have been Pioneer 10 and 11, and Voyager 1 and 2. Since their launch in the 1970s, a torrent of priceless information has poured back to us on Earth.

Voyager 2 photographs Saturn

Will we ever live on another planet? Both the United States and Russia have plans for human settlements on Mars—but space probes are expected to pave the way, by dropping an army of robot explorers.

Mariner 10 over Mercury

The **Young Observer** *Quiz*

1. Who is carrying a message for aliens?
a) The mailman?
b) The space shuttle?
c) The Pioneer probes?

FOR SALE

5. What happened to Skylab?
Did it:
a) Fly off into space?
b) Crash back to Earth?
c) Land safely on Earth?

2. Who sent messages from Mars?
a) A Martian?
b) A Viking?
c) A Norman?

6. How do astronauts go to the bathroom?
Do they:
a) Wait until they return to Earth?
b) Use a special toilet?
c) Use a normal toilet?

7. How do astronauts prepare their food?

3. What keeps satellites in orbit?
a) Rockets?
b) Solar panels?
c) Earth's gravity?

Do they:
a) Use a stove?
b) Eat cold food?
c) Go on a diet?

4. Who spies from space?
a) Satellites?
b) Spies in spacesuits?
c) Aliens?

8. Where is the space probe Voyager 1 now?
a) On Pluto?
b) In deep space?
c) In a museum?

ANSWERS ON PAGES 36–37

The **Answers** to Chapter One (PAGE 13)

1. How many Earths will fit into the Sun?

Answer: c)

The Sun looks small from Earth, but that's because it is so far away —about 93 million miles! The Sun is vast, of course. Its diameter is nearly 860,000 miles—109 times that of Earth. Well over a million Earths could fit inside it.

2. How hot is the Sun?

Answer: a) and b)

The Sun's heat is generated by nuclear reactions in its superhot core. The temperature here reaches a staggering 27 million °F. It can take as long as a million years for this heat to move up through the Sun's layers to its surface, the photosphere, where the temperature is about 10,000 °F—this is still hot enough to make solid iron bars boil away into clouds of gas!

3. How fast can a comet travel?

Answer: b)

All comets travel at different speeds, and they are fastest when their orbits bring them close to the Sun. Halley's Comet averages 150,000 miles per hour. No comet reaches speeds greater than 1,476,000 miles per hour.

PHOTOSPHERE

CONVECTIVE LAYER

RADIATIVE LAYER

CORE

4. What's the heaviest surviving meteorite to have hit the Earth?

Answer: b)

The largest known meteorite lies where it fell to Earth thousands of years ago—at Hoba West in Namibia, Africa. It weighs a massive 60 tons. Meteor Crater, in Arizona, is 560 feet deep and was probably created by a meteorite about 150 feet wide.

5. Where are we in this picture of our galaxy?

Answer: a)
Just in case you get lost in outer space—we live on one of the Milky Way's spiraling arms, about 28,000 light-years from the center! From one side to the other, our galaxy measures about 100,000 light-years. It looks like a giant pinwheel.

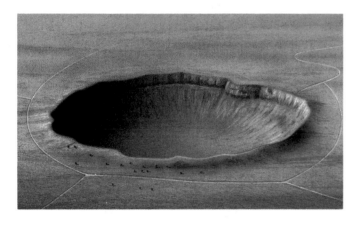

6 How many asteroids are there?

Answer: a) and c)
There are millions of chunks of rock in the asteroid belt between Mars and Jupiter. Just over 5,000 have been named. There are also other, smaller asteroid groups which follow different orbits.

7. What is a light-year?

Answer: b)
A light-year is the distance a ray of light travels through space in one year. Light travels at about 186,000 miles per second, and a light-year is around 5.88 million million miles. When we look at a star that is 100 light-years away, we are seeing it as it was 100 years ago—the time its light has taken to reach us.

8. Where can you find a horse's head in space?

Answer: c)
The Horsehead Nebula is in the star-group of Orion. The horse's head is a dark cloud of cool gas and dust, which stands out against the bright light of newly-formed stars beyond it.

The **Answers** to Chapter Two (PAGE 21)

1. Which planet is closest in size to Earth?

Answer: b)
Check the planet facts on these pages and you will see that it's Venus, which is also our nearest neighbor. Differences between us include the fact that Venus spins in a clockwise direction—the opposite way from Earth.

KEY
Planet's name
Distance from Sun
Diameter
Number of moons
Period of rotation
Orbital period

Mercury
36 million miles
3,030 miles
0
58 days 16 hrs.
88 days

Venus
67 million miles
7,545 miles
0
243 days 14 min.
225 days

2. Which planet is named after the god of war?

Answer: c)
Mars was the name the Romans gave to their god of war. The planet was named after him because its red glow in the night sky reminded people of blood. All the planets, except our own Earth, are named after Greek or Roman gods and goddesses.

3. Where is a "day" longer than a year?

Answer: c)
Venusians—if there were any—would celebrate their first birthday before they were one day old! Venus takes longer to spin around once than it does to orbit the Sun. Its period of rotation is 243 Earth-days. Its orbital period, or "year," is a fraction under 225 Earth-days.

Orbital period
Sun
Period of rotation

Earth
93 million miles
7,926 miles
1
23 hrs. 56 min.
365 days

Mars
142 million miles
4,220 miles
2
24 hrs. 37 min.
687 days

Jupiter
483 million miles
88,700 miles
16
9 hrs. 55 min.
11.9 years

Venus
Goddess of Love

Jupiter
King of the gods

Uranus
God of the Heavens

Pluto God of the Underworld

Mercury
Messenger of the gods

Mars
God of War

Saturn
God of Farming

Neptune
God of the Sea

4. Which planet was bombed by a comet in 1994?

Answer: a)

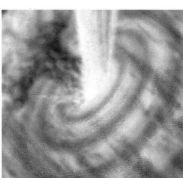

Jupiter's gravity sucked in a passing comet called Shoemaker-Levy, which then broke up into huge chunks. The collisions were spectacular as these punched into Jupiter's atmosphere.

5. Which moons' names mean "fear" and "terror"?

Answer: c)

Do you speak ancient Greek? No? Well, Phobos means "fear" and Deimos means "terror" in Greek. They are those little potato-shaped moons that spin around Mars—tiny worlds of cratered and scarred black rock.

6. Which planet may not really be a planet?

Answer: c)

Pluto was called a planet when it was discovered in 1930, but some astronomers are beginning to wonder.... Pluto is more like a moon than a planet, and it is strange to find a rocky planet so far from the Sun —Pluto's neighbors are the four gas giants.

Pluto
3,660 million miles
1,430 miles
1
6 days 9 hrs.
248.5 years

Neptune
2,799 million miles
30,000 miles
8
19 hrs. 12 min.
164.8 years

Uranus
1,783 million miles
32,300 miles
15
17 hrs. 54 min.
84 years

Saturn
887 million miles
75,000 miles
18
10 hrs. 40 min.
29.5 years

Neptune

Sun

Pluto

7. Which planet is farthest from the Sun?

Answer: b) and c)

Between 1979 and 1999 (and for 20 years of every 248.5-year orbit), Pluto is closer to the Sun than Neptune.

8. On which planet do winds reach 1,200 mph?

Answer: a)

Neptune is the windiest planet.

The **Answers** to Chapter Three (PAGE 31)

1. Who is carrying a message for aliens?

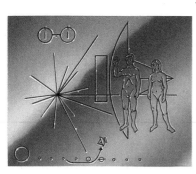

Answer: c)
A special picture was attached to the probes Pioneer 10 and 11 before they started their long trek through the solar system. It showed a man and a woman, and a diagram giving Earth's position in the solar system—just in case there are any alien beings out there who might find it....

2. Who sent messages from Mars?

Answer: b)
Two Viking landers were sent down to the surface of Mars in 1976. Between them, they sent back 3,000 images as well as measuring wind speed and temperature, and carrying out tests on Martian soil. But they didn't find any signs of life!

A Viking lander

3. What keeps satellites in orbit?

Answer: c)
Once a satellite has been launched into orbit by a rocket or space shuttle,

Gyroscopes check the satellite is the right way up.

Gas thrusters keep the satellite on course.

it is held in position by Earth's gravity. However, power is still needed to control the height, course, and speed of the satellite's orbit. Gas thrusters (controlled by computer from Earth) are used to maneuver it, while gyroscopes monitor its balance and solar panels provide electrical power.

Solar panels convert the Sun's energy into electrical power.

4. Who spies from space?

Answer: a)

A hundred years ago, armies sent up spies in hot-air balloons to draw pictures of the enemy's position and weapons. Today, special spy satellites are sent into orbit. These can photograph movements of troops, tanks, or rocket-launchers —every detail of enemy activity. Spy satellites have sharp enough "eye-sight" to see car license plates!

geostationary orbit

5. What happened to Skylab?

Answer: b)

On July 11, 1979, the U.S. space station Skylab reentered Earth's atmosphere. It burned up over the Indian Ocean and pieces of it rained down over the West Australia coast. Fortunately nobody was hurt, not even a kangaroo!

6. How do astronauts go to the bathroom?

Answer: b)

The first astronauts wore collecting bags, but Mir and the space shuttle have special toilets. The toilets are quite comfortable, but weightlessness means that astronauts have to pull a bar across their legs to stop themselves floating off the seat. A flow of air sucks away the waste, which is dried.

7. How do astronauts prepare their food?

Answer: a) and b)

Space meals are precooked and packaged in sealed containers. They can be eaten cold or warmed in an oven. Drinks are sucked through a special straw.

8. Where is the space probe Voyager 1 now?

Answer: b)

All the Pioneer and Voyager space probes have now left the solar system and are heading out into deep space. Pioneer 10 is the farthest from home.

USEFUL WORDS

ASTEROID *One of the millions of small rocky bodies orbiting the Sun. More than 90 percent of asteroids are found between Mars and Jupiter.*

ASTRONOMER *Someone who studies the stars and other heavenly bodies.*

ATMOSPHERE *The layer of gases around a planet (its "air"), which is held down by gravity. Earth's atmosphere is mainly nitrogen and oxygen gas. Smaller bodies with weak gravity, such as the Moon, have no atmosphere.*

AXIS *The imaginary line through the center of a star, planet, or moon, around which it spins.*

BLACK HOLE *A space object with such strong gravity that nothing can escape from it, not even light.*

COMET *One of billions of balls of snow and dust (miles in diameter) that orbit the Sun.*

CORE *The center of a planet or star.*

COSMOLOGIST *Somebody who studies the universe—how it began, its history, and what may happen to it.*

DWARF STAR *Either an ordinary "small" dim star, or the dying remains of a bright star (white or brown dwarf).*

ECLIPSE *There are two kinds of eclipse. An eclipse of the Sun happens if the Moon's orbit takes it directly between the Earth and the Sun. An eclipse of the Moon takes place if the full moon passes directly through the Earth's shadow. The Moon turns a reddish-brown color.*

GALAXY *A vast number of stars held together by gravity.*

GIANT STAR *Either a star that is hotter and brighter than our Sun (white or blue giant), or an old star that has begun to expand and cool when it has used up its hydrogen fuel (red giant).*

GRAVITY *Every object in the universe has this pulling force. The more massive the object, the stronger its gravity. The Earth's gravity keeps our feet on the ground and stops us floating into space, while the Sun's much stronger gravity holds the Earth in orbit around it.*

METEOR *The streak of light seen when a meteoroid (a small piece of space rock) burns up in the Earth's atmosphere.*
METEORITE *A meteoroid (see METEOR) that hits the ground because it is too big to burn up.*

NEBULA *A huge cloud of gas and dust in a galaxy. Stars are born inside nebulae.*

NEUTRON STAR *The hot ball of solid material which is all that remains after a giant star explodes in a supernova.*

NUCLEAR REACTION *All substances are made up of invisibly tiny atoms, and the nucleus at the center of each atom contains huge amounts of energy. A nuclear reaction is when the nucleus of an atom is changed in some way (by the heat inside a star, for example), releasing some of its energy as heat and light.*

ORBIT *The curved path of something that travels around a star or planet. Each planet, including Earth, has its own orbit around the Sun.*

POLES *The two opposite points on the surface of a spinning star, planet, or moon, where the axis passes through it.*

ROCKET *A machine that burns fuel to produce hot gases. As the gases shoot out backward, they thrust the rocket forward or upward at great speed. Space rockets carry tanks of liquid fuel (often hydrogen) and oxygen. Oxygen is needed because things will not burn without it.*

SATELLITE *Anything that orbits a planet. Moons are natural satellites. Artificial (man-made) satellites are spacecraft that orbit the Earth.*

SOLAR SYSTEM *Our Sun, and the comets, asteroids, nine planets, and their moons that orbit it.*

SPACE PROBE *A crewless spacecraft that leaves the Earth's orbit to explore other planets and moons, comets, and asteroids.*

SUPERGIANT *A really massive star, hundreds of times bigger than our Sun.*

SUPERNOVA *The colossal explosion that destroys a giant star. A neutron star or a black hole may be all that is left after a supernova.*

TELESCOPE *An instrument for studying distant objects, such as planets or stars. Optical telescopes work by gathering the light from distant objects, and focusing it through lenses and by mirrors. Radio telescopes have huge dishes that collect radio signals given off by distant space bodies.*

UNIVERSE *The whole of space and everything it contains.*

INDEX